The Heart of a Lioness

Gargi Sonawane

NEEMTREE
Publishing House

The Heart of a Lioness

First published in Nov 2024 by

Neemtree Publishing House

Email: contact@neemtreelabs.com

www.neemtreelabs.com

Author: Gargi Sonawane

Cover by: Veerendra Tikhe

Layout and Design: Sanganak Prakshan

P ISBN: 978-81-981540-7-1

E ISBN: 978-81-981540-2-6

TABLE OF CONTENTS

TABLE OF CONTENTS

Author's Note:

This book is a collection of poems that depicts the story of a female warrior, and her journey of how she overcomes all the obstacles in her path, to emerge victorious, in this never-ending battle called life. My aim behind writing this book is to empower all women who think they are any less. Despite living in the so-called modern era of the 21st century, it is sad to see that gender discrimination is still so prevalent today especially in the rural areas wherein the patriarchal mindset is extremely predominant. I am lucky to be born in a family where my education and upbringing are given importance, my voice and opinions are respected and my talent appreciated. However, this is certainly not the case with other unfortunate women who have been subjected to domestic violence, sexual harassment, and child marriage. Some women are slain by their own families in the name of honour killings. On the other hand, some are not even given a chance to take their first breath due to a simple cultural preference towards male children. It is truly sad to witness such tragedies despite living in a 'progressive' human civilization. What's even worse is that women themselves don't think they have the right to speak up and fight against this social evil that destroys the lives of countless woman even today. It is crucial that we raise our voices and fight. Fight against this degenerative mentality and eradicate gender inequality. My goal behind writing this book is to inspire and empower all women through a beautiful and powerful story now presented before you...

Chapter 1
Love beyond Blood

| A warrior is born

The tale of a warrior queen,
Born with the heart of a lioness,
A story neither told nor seen,
Let me show you what I truly mean.

It was a dark night,
Thunder, lightning, and horrifying storms,
A ray of light was born to a brave knight,
At the birth of a girl, her father storms.

Abandoned by those who gave birth,
Thrown into the Gale river within a basket,
Taken to Valandor by mother earth,
Adopted by royals who truly saw her worth.

Amara, Valandor's queen,
Teared up looking at this innocent life,
Childless for years, this was her dream,
She thanked the majestic Gale stream.

Rushing towards Aric her king,
She says exuberantly,
"To you, look whom I bring,"
Aric's face lights up as the new spring.

"Kiara" Aric says,
The one who lit up his life,
The answer to all his prays,
"Today is the best among all days."

| Why can't Kiara Rule?

Kiara, her beauty was unparalleled,
With a sharp intellect and unwavering focus,
As a warrior and in studies she excelled,
Kindness in her heart, always dwelled.

Adored by the subjects of her kingdom,
Loved most by her mother,
Known for her unmatched wisdom,
Her values were like none other.

Taught warfare in secrecy by her mother Amara,
Brought up as a true warrior,
She became the best fighter of her Era,
Her birth was no longer a barrier.

She always had a dream, a spark in her eyes,
To rule Valandor righteously,
But Aric constantly denies,
Yet, her dreams touch the skies.

Kiara says to Aric in a hopeful tone,
"No one is more worthy than me to rule,"
"If not me, who will ascend the throne?"
"Come on, don't be so cruel."

Aric says "It's family tradition,"
"There's nothing I can do"
"Please don't put me in this position"
"Women can't lead, that is what's true."

| Fate of the queen

It was a dark night once again,
The thunder rumbled a warning,
The skies were crying in pain,
Perhaps the fate of the queen was daunting.

Frightened by the lightning strikes,
A 13-year-old Kiara visits her mother,
Amara nowhere to be found; to Kiara it strikes,
The floor was covered with laser sharp spikes.

Drops of blood spilled all over,
A terrified Kiara screams in fear,
Aric comes and says "take cover,"
Handing Kiara a spear.

Quietly hiding inside Amara's closet,
She sees her mother racing towards her,
Handing Kiara her precious locket,
Little did Kiara know; Amara was the target.

Delighted to be reunited,
Kiara gives Amara a tight hug,
Evident in her eyes, Amara was frightened,
The tension in the atmosphere heightened.

Just before Amara revealed the truth,
An arrow pierced through her chest,
Scarring Kiara's youth,
Amara, forever had left.

Chapter 2

The Cost of Victory

| Aric Finds Out!

Aric tries a million times,
Amara's killer is nowhere to be found,
After witnessing the worst of crimes,
Aric grows bitter as unripe limes.

Devastated by her mother's death,
Kiara makes a resolve,
She will not give up until her last breath,
This mystery, she must solve.

Until then Kiara diverts herself,
Focusing on her rigorous training,
Reading all the scriptures in the royal bookshelf,
Training without complaining.

At the age of 17 her skills are unmatched,
Aric is enraged upon finding out,
Kiara's weapons he snatched,
Purposeless, she finds herself filled with doubt.

Furious, Aric decides to get Kiara married,
Searching for suitors across distant lands,
Until then, the weight of the kingdom Aric carried,
While Kiara's dreams are deeply buried.

After months of searching,
Aric finds no one worthy for his daughter,
Still unable to train, Kiara was hurting,
Not yet recovered from her mother's slaughter.

| Time for War

Unable to find Kiara a match,
Aric becomes frustrated,
He lets her learn warfare, but there's a catch,
Once he finds a suitor she will be obligated.

Despite a million tries,
He finds no one worthy,
Meanwhile, Kiara tries to vocalize,
Still recovering from her mother's demise.

Aric finally decides to give up,
Much to his daughter's delight,
She was at last relieved from her plight,
With Aric she no longer had to fight.

A few days pass away,
Valandor, sees the dawn of good days,
But this good time was not to stay,
Destiny had its own plans anyways.

Valandor, a kingdom rarely attacked,
The time for war had unfortunately come,
Kiara had her weapons all ready and stacked,
Aric unaware of the warrior she had become.

Ready to fight with all her might,
Kiara wields her sword and steps outside,
Just when Aric says "You cannot fight,"
"In war women don't have the right."

| Aric in War

Shattered completely,
Kiara is disheartened,
By her father's sharp words, wounded deeply,
Her days in the palace darkened.

There was nothing she could do,
When the kingdom needed her most,
Nothing had made her this blue,
What is happening in the war, she had no clue.

The enemy set the kingdom on fire,
The land entirely devastated,
Kiara couldn't protect her subjects, her only desire,
Her talent, completely wasted.

Meanwhile Aric enters the battle,
The enemy's army is twice as his,
His feet out of fear begin to rattle,
Him not much of a warrior, as his daughter is.

Still, he gathers all the courage,
Lifts the sword with all his might,
Frees his soldiers under enemy hostage,
Ferociously continuing to fight.

Despite having a smaller one,
Aric destroys the enemy's army,
The opposing chief commander is in complete stun.
As his soldiers begin to run.

| An Attack from Behind

Overtaken by vanity,
Aric becomes unalert,
Unaware of the future calamity,
About to be severely hurt.

The opposing chief commander approaches Aric,
Against the rules, from behind,
For evil powers this is a classic,
The commander plays with Aric's mind.

An excellent archer,
The commander fixes his target,
For Kiara what punishment could be harsher,
Her life keeps getting darker.

The commander shoots the arrow,
Which pierces through Aric's Armor,
How can a person be so shallow?
Valandor's worst harmer.

Blood dripping from his chest,
Tears pouring from his eyes,
Aric doesn't take a moment to rest,
He must finish the war that's left.

He pulls out the arrow from his body,
Gives the commander a fearless look,
He looked hurt, hardly,
As his courage was still unshook.

| Victory's Effect

Aric once again wielded his weapon,
Approached the commander fiercely,
He was shot with arrows one by one,
Aric pulled them out repeatedly.

Frightened by Aric's courage,
The commander decides to retrieve,
Having received his King's message,
He doesn't take a moment to leave.

Having won the war,
Aric returns victoriously,
Never been wounded so gravely before,
Can he survive some time more?

Upon seeing her father return,
Kiara's eyes are filled with tears,
Feeling a myriad of emotions she cannot discern,
Seeing Aric this injured, her heart does burn.

Aric faints as he steps into the palace,
Kiara rushes to help him,
Realizing the war was extremely disastrous,
The hope for Valandor becomes dim.

Kiara steps out to see her subjects,
The kingdom is completely devastated,
Are these victory's effects?
Kiara looking at Aric reflects.

Chapter 3

A Mother's Legacy

| The Secret Diary

Aric's condition deteriorates,
As he lies on his death bed,
Valandor further degenerates,
For her father Kiara dreads.

Devastated, she enters Amara's room,
Searching inside her closet for memories,
Hoping to outlive her doom,
But then something unexpected she sees.

She discovers Amara's secret diary,
Hesitant at first, Kiara flips its pages,
After reading some, she is shocked entirely,
Kiara waited for this breakthrough since ages.

Secrets that Kiara never knew were revealed,
Let's take a moment to see Amara's past,
Look at the stories deliberately concealed,
The reason why Amara had passed.

Amara was just like Kiara in her youth,
With kings lined up to marry her,
Amara through their eyes could see the truth,
Couldn't be fooled, her thoughts were always clear.

Among those kings was Drake,
A wealthy and arrogant prince,
His personality, completely fake
Amara he failed to convince.

| Amara's Past Revealed

Mesmerized by her beauty,
Madly in love with Amara,
She rejects him rudely,
Drake was enraged absolutely.

Amara fell in love with Aric,
Their marriage was soon fixed,
Drake's reaction was completely hysteric,
Amara's emotions slightly mixed.

On the marriage day Drake vows,
He will not let Amara live in peace,
Feelings of rage in Drake arouse,
This day, Drake from his mind will never release.

Even years after her marriage,
Drake would send threat notes,
To tell Aric, Amara couldn't find the courage,
These notes, in her Diary Amara notes.

Amara taught Kiara to fight,
As she suspected Drake to attack,
Although she knew Aric with this, wasn't alright,
She had to do something when Drake was back.

One final day,
Drake sent Amara a death threat,
Telling her she couldn't get away,
Hoping her decision she would regret.

| **Aric is Gone**

Suspecting Drake to be Amara's killer,
Kiara sends spies to find out,
After confirming, she grows even bitter,
She must avenge her mother without doubt.

A few moments later,
Aric screams in pain,
Waiting for his daughter,
Patience he could not maintain.

Racing towards her father,
Kiara is frightened,
It's like the distance between them increases farther,
The severity of Aric's condition heightened.

With tears in her eyes,
Kiara finally reaches her father,
Knowing death is close Aric cries,
To live a few moments more he tries harder.

Aric kisses Kiara's forehead,
Saying his final goodbyes,
Precious Tears they shed,
Thereafter he dies.

Kiara is frozen in shock,
Lost both her adoptive parents,
Her heart becomes hard as rock.
It's certainly not her time on the clock.

| Valandor's new Queen

Kiara was completely shattered,
And so was the kingdom without a ruler,
All her emotions Kiara gathered,
And thought about Valandor's future.

The courtiers began to fight,
As to who would ascend the royal throne,
All to Kiara's plight,
She was being overthrown.

With courage in her heart,
And her purpose in mind,
Kiara decides to fulfil her part,
Leaving her misery behind.

She approaches the courtiers and says assertively,
"I am Valandor's new queen,"
The courtiers burst into laughter,
As a female ruler they had never seen.

Kiara is enraged,
She gives them a ferocious stare,
The gravity of her words they gauged,
Of her worthiness still unaware.

An unloyal courtier attacks her from behind,
She grabs a sword and cuts his head,
Fierce and fearless their new queen they find,
A true warrior - one of a kind.

Chapter 4
Courage Ignited

| To be Attacked

After displaying her might,
The courtiers accept Kiara as their ruler,
She had fought for what's right,
Taking in her hands, Valandor's future.

The next day a messenger brings shocking news,
Drake is attacking Valandor again,
To give up she does refuse,
She must take revenge for her mother's pain.

Drake decides to attack,
Knowing that Aric has passed away,
Kiara is determined to fight back,
"Let us surrender" the courtiers say.

Knowing that if Drake rules,
Valandor will become like hell,
With an inspiring speech she reveals Amara's past,
In their hearts now, rage and courage dwell.

They start preparing for war,
But the resources are insufficient,
The army is much smaller than before,
Against Drake they may fall deficient.

Kiara must come up with a solution,
Lead her kingdom to victory,
In the army she brings a revolution,
Something never done in history.

| **Women and Weapons**

Drake's army was thrice as larger,
Weapons he had plenty,
Defeating him was becoming harder,
Valandor's royal treasury, almost empty.

Kiara ordered all her subjects to gather,
Filling them with inspiration,
Convincing them to fight for what will truly matter,
The well-being of their nation.

The citizens join the army,
Still unmatched with the enemy,
Kiara must act fast,
Else, in the war they won't last.

She orders women of the kingdom,
To come together,
Empowers them to fight against the unjust system,
Convinces them to join this endeavour.

Another problem she must solve,
The weaponry is not enough,
In Kiara's mind ideas evolve,
After which it ceases to be tough.

She creates new and more powerful weapons,
Using the resources already present,
The courtiers realize their misconceptions,
For Drake this war won't be very pleasant.

| **The Beginning of War**

She reveals Amara's past,
To all her army,
The reason why Amara had passed,
Their patience now did not last.

Kiara trains the female warriors,
To be skilled and courageous,
Impressing the courtiers,
Remembering Drake's actions as outrageous.

With a futuristic vision,
She devises better weapons,
To fulfil her mission,
Only she could take such a decision.

With fire in their eyes,
And courage in their hearts,
The people of Valandor arise,
The war finally starts.

Chapter 5

Hope on the Brink

| **About to Lose**

The war had officially begun,
Kiara as always fighting ferociously,
As if she and the sword were one,
Destroying the enemy heroically.

Individually she was undefeated,
But her soldiers not nearly the same,
Her army quickly depleted,
As the leader, is Kiara the one to blame?

The death of so many subjects especially women,
Her decision for a moment she regrets,
Perhaps to Aric she should listen,
Kiara was troubled to see these bloodsheds.

She falls on her knees,
About to give up and loose
But then Amara's locket she sees,
And remembers her roots.

Unable to gather the courage before,
Now she opens the locket,
Her hope, the locket will restore,
The moment she will unlock it.

'Fearless Hearts, Unbreakable Spirits,'
By the locket's message Kiara is empowered,
The higher purpose she revisits,
Her mother's blessings over her showered.

| Chief Commander is Dead

Her courage is regained,
Kiara stands firmly wielding her sword,
She freed her soldiers that were chained,
To lose hope, now she couldn't afford.

Seeing the commander who attacked Aric,
She challenges him for a duel,
The chief commander is amused,
While fighting, Kiara's hand was bruised.

Yet she fought ferociously,
Finally destroyed the commander,
Kiara kills him heroically,
Her soldiers then truly admired her.

The courage of her soldiers was restored,
The enemy's army scared at their commander's death,
They feared Kiara's sword,
As she vows to fight until her last breath.

She finally spots her mother's killer,
Drake, her sworn enemy,
She gives him a look that's bitter,
As she recalls that dark night memory.

She approaches Drake,
And says fearlessly,
"For my mother and Valandor's sake,"
"I will kill you as you did my mother shamelessly."

| **A Duel with Drake**

Realizing she is Amara's daughter,
Aric gives an evil smile,
Bursting out into a cunning laughter,
Thinking this duel will be worthwhile.

Challenging Drake to a duel,
Kiara begins to fight,
In the duel, Drake is just as cruel,
Kiara fights for what's right.

A 7 feet tall Drake,
Much more powerful,
Kiara is now fully awake,
Drake as usual is dreadful.

Kiara not as experienced,
Smaller in size, and not that strong,
A fierce duel she experienced,
Fighting against what's wrong.

She took a moment to think carefully,
She may not have the strength,
But could rely on her intellect primarily,
Her speed and agility overpower Drake's length.

She pulls an acrobatic stunt,
And Drake is fooled to look behind,
She attacks him from the front,
Playing with his mind.

| Kiara is Shocked

With all her might, still in air,
Kiara cuts Drake's body in half,
Drake's Army in complete despair,
Kiara has taken revenge on Amara's Behalf.

Falling on her knees,
Kiara begins to cry,
For the flashback of her life she sees,
She looks up at the clear sky.

Shocked by the fact,
That she had won the war,
With her army still intact,
This war was like never before.

The battlefield echoes,
With the sound of a loud applause,
For the victory over foes,
Knowing Kiara was the cause.

| **The Lioness Roars**

With the heart of a lioness,
And the vision of an eagle,
Kiara works in a manner tireless,
Constantly fighting, against all evil.

Everyone realizes,
Being a woman is not a limitation,
After Kiara, as a queen rises,
Righteously, ruling the Valandor Nation.

An epitome of women empowerment,
She teaches us, women are no less,
For the world's betterment,
On this issue, we must raise awareness.